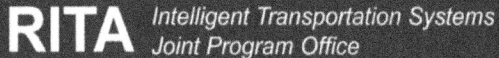 **RITA** *Intelligent Transportation Systems*
Joint Program Office

Vehicle Information Exchange Needs for Mobility Applications

www.its.dot.gov/index.htm
Final Report — February 13, 2012
FHWA-JPO-12-021

U.S. Department of Transportation

Research and Innovative Technology
Administration

Produced by Name of Contract
ITS Joint Program Office
Research and Innovative Technology Administration
U.S. Department of Transportation

Technical Report Documentation Page

1. Report No. FHWA-JPO-12-021	2. Government Accession No.	3. Recipient's Catalog No.	
4. Title and Subtitle Vehicle Information Exchange Needs for Mobility ApplicationsExchange		5. Report Date February 13, 2012	
		6. Performing Organization Code	
7. Author(s) Michael McGurrin		8. Performing Organization Report No.	
9. Performing Organization Name And Address Noblis, 600 Maryland Avenue, SW, Suite 755, Washington, DC 20024		10. Work Unit No. (TRAIS)	
		11. Contract or Grant No. DTFH61-11-D-00018	
12. Sponsoring Agency Name and Address United States Department of Transportation Research and Innovative Technology Administration Intelligent Transportation System Joint Program Office 1200 New Jersey Avenue, S.E. Washington, DC 20590		13. Type of Report and Period Covered Version 1.0	
		14. Sponsoring Agency Code USDOT RITA JPO	

15. Supplementary Notes

16. Abstract

Connected Vehicle to Vehicle (V2V) safety applications heavily rely on the BSM, which is one of the messages defined in the Society of Automotive standard J2735, Dedicated Short Range Communications (DSRC) Message Set Dictionary, November 2009. The BSM is broadcast from vehicles over the 5.9 GHz DSRC band. Transmission range is on the order of 1,000 meters. The BSM consists of two parts:

- BSM Part 1:
  - Contains core data elements, including vehicle position, heading, speed, acceleration, steering wheel angle, and vehicle size
  - It is transmitted at an adjustable rate of about 10 times per second
- BSM Part 2:
  - Contains a variable set of data elements drawn from an extensive list of optional elements. They are selected based on event triggers, e.g., ABS activated
  - They are added to Part 1 and sent as part of the BSM message, but are transmitted less frequently in order to conserve bandwidth

The BSM message includes only current snapshots (with the exception of path data which is itself limited to a few second's worth of past history data).

A preliminary assessment of the information that needs to flow to and from vehicles in order to support thirty high priority applications identified by the Dynamic Mobility Applications (DMA) program was conducted to determine the extent to which the Basic Safety Message (BSM) can support those needs. The concepts of operation and system requirements for these DMA applications are still under development. As a result, the findings will undoubtedly change as more information becomes available.

The primary findings of the analysis are:
1. The Basic Safety Message (BSM), with Part 1 transmitted approximately 10 times per second over Dedicated Short Range Communications (DSRC), is useful for a limited subset of mobility applications, but is not solely sufficient for most applications, especially since complete roadway coverage using DSRC has never been envisioned as a feasible option.
2. A subset of the BSM Part 1 and Part 2 data, if cached, bundled, and sent in another manner (e.g., periodic transmission of both current and history data over cellular networks), adequately provides the vehicle-based information needed for most mobility applications. The major exception is crash-related data to support the MAYDAY application.

17. Key Words Connected vehicles, Basic Safety Message, BSM, mobility applications, Dynamic Mobility Applications, DMA		18. Distribution Statement	
19. Security Classif. (of this report)	20. Security Classif. (of this page)	21. No. of Pages 47	22. Price

Table of Contents

List of Tables

List of Figures

Executive Summary

This white paper presents the results of a preliminary assessment of the information that needs to flow to and from vehicles in order to support thirty high priority applications identified by the Dynamic Mobility Applications (DMA) program and the extent to which the Basic Safety Message (BSM) can support those needs. The concepts of operation and system requirements for these DMA applications are still under development. As a result, the findings will undoubtedly change as more information becomes available. This document will be periodically updated through mid-2013.

Connected Vehicle to Vehicle (V2V) safety applications heavily rely on the BSM, which is one of the messages defined in the Society of Automotive standard J2735, *Dedicated Short Range Communications (DSRC) Message Set Dictionary*, November 2009. The BSM is broadcast from vehicles over the 5.9 GHz DSRC band. Transmission range is on the order of 1,000 meters. The BSM consists of two parts:

- BSM Part 1:
  - Contains core data elements, including vehicle position, heading, speed, acceleration, steering wheel angle, and vehicle size
  - It is transmitted at an adjustable rate of about 10 times per second

- BSM Part 2:
  - Contains a variable set of data elements drawn from an extensive list of optional elements. They are selected based on event triggers, e.g., ABS activated
  - They are added to Part 1 and sent as part of the BSM message, but are transmitted less frequently in order to conserve bandwidth

The BSM message includes only current snapshots (with the exception of path data which is itself limited to a few second's worth of past history data).

The primary findings of the analysis are:

1. *The Basic Safety Message (BSM), with Part 1 transmitted approximately 10 times per second over Dedicated Short Range Communications (DSRC), is useful for a limited subset of mobility applications, but is not solely sufficient for most applications, especially since complete roadway coverage using DSRC has never been envisioned as a feasible option.*
2. *A subset of the BSM Part 1 and Part 2 data, if cached, bundled, and sent in another manner (e.g., periodic transmission of both current and history data over cellular networks), adequately provides the vehicle-based information needed for most mobility applications. The major exception is crash-related data to support the MAYDAY application.*

A subset of the mobility applications can utilize the BSM as currently defined and broadcast. Other mobility applications require the information in parts 1 and 2 of the BSM, but not at 10 times per second broadcast over DSRC. The data is often needed for every stretch of roadway, but far less frequently. Since it is infeasible to provide ubiquitous coverage of U.S. roadways using DSRC, the data must be cached on-board the vehicle and then sent in a message containing both current and stored snapshots. These new messages could be sent to roadside DSRC units spaced along the roadway, as in the original Vehicle Infrastructure Integration (VII) vision, sent via digital cellular, or through a combination of the two.

The BSM data elements that are most widely used by mobility applications, albeit not in a 10 Hz BSM message, are the vehicle parameters found in Part 1 of the BSM and weather related data found in Part 2 of the BSM. This is shown in Table 0-1.

Table 0-1. BSM Data Elements Used by the Largest Number of Mobility Applications

BSM Part 1	BSM Part 2
Position (local 3D): • Latitude • Longitude • Elevation • Positional accuracy	Road coefficient of friction
Motion: • Transmission state • Speed • Heading • Steering wheel angle • Acceleration Set (4-way): this includes 3 axes of acceleration plus yaw rate	Rain sensor (called a Rain sensor in J2735, but it is a precipitation sensor. J2735 states "The "Rain Sensor" Probe Data Element is intended to inform Probe Data Users as to how hard it was raining/snowing…")
Vehicle size	Traction Control System active over 100 msec
	Antilock Brake System active over 100 msec
	Lights changed and Exterior lights (status)
	Wipers changed and wiper status
	Ambient air temperature
	Ambient air pressure
	Vehicle type (BSM currently only includes this for fleet vehicles)

There are two additional sets of vehicle information that are not found in either Part 1 or Part 2 of the BSM but that may be of value to particular applications. First, the Mayday Relay and Incident Scene Pre-Arrival Staging and Guidance for Emergency Responders applications would benefit from crash-related data from the vehicle. Second, although outside the scope of this study, AERIS applications may derive value from additional variables such as fuel consumption and fuel efficiency. [Note: The Connected Eco Driving (ECO) application that is part of the Mulitpmodal Intelligent Traffic Signal Sytem (M-ISIG) bundle was included in the analysis, however as currently defined it does not require that information be sent from the vehicle]

It is important to note two additional items. First, with respect to BSM messages, the fact that a data element is defined as an element of Part 2 of the BSM in the Society of Automotive Engineers (SAE)

J2735 standard does not necessarily mean that it will be provided by vehicle manufacturers. Most of the Part 2 elements are defined as optional information in the standard. Second, while this paper focusses on data from vehicles, it is important to keep in mind that transformative mobility applications will require data from travelers and other sensors, in addition to vehicle data.

Chapter 1: Introduction

Purpose

This white paper presents the results of a preliminary assessment of the information that needs to flow to and from vehicles in order to support the high priority mobility applications.[1] One of the principal goals of the assessment was to assess the extent to which the information found in Part 1 and Part 2 of the Basic Safety Message (BSM) parts 1 and 2 is sufficient to enable the set of mobility applications. This paper is intended to provide preliminary answers to four questions:

- To what degree does Part 1 of the BSM, transmitted using Dedicated Short Range Communications (DSRC) meet the needs of the mobility applications?

- Which data elements in parts 1 and 2 of the BSM are needed for mobility applications?

- If BSM data is only sent via DSRC, what extent of DSRC infrastructure is needed to support mobility applications

- What other data, not found in the BSM messages, must be sent to and from vehicles to support mobility applications?

The study was conducted to address a time-critical need for a qualitative assessment. The analysis is highly preliminary. The concepts of operations for the various applications have not yet been developed. For several of the applications, there are differing concepts of vehicle or infrastructure-base systems, with very different information exchange needs. The needs will be revisited as work on the concepts of operation and system requirements are developed for each application. This document will be periodically updated through mid-2013.

Background

The National Highway Traffic Safety Administration (NHTSA) has announced that they will make a decision in 2013 on whether or not to move forward with rulemaking that would require future vehicles to support Vehicle to Vehicle (V2V) and Vehicle to Infrastructure (V2I) data communications for safety applications. The essential information required for V2V safety applications has been standardized in the Basic Safety Message parts 1 and 2. It is envisioned that each equipped vehicle will broadcast Part 1 of the BSM over a DSRC channel, at an adjustable rate of approximately 10 times per second.

---

[1] Based on recommendations from stakeholders and USDOT staff, an assessment of deployment readiness, and the prospective federal role, a set of 30 "high priority mobility applications" was developed as part of the connected vehicle mobility program. A summary of these applications can be found at http://www.its.dot.gov/dma/pdf/MAP-HP%20V5.3%20F.pdf. These applications, listed in Appendix C, cover freeway, arterial, regional information, and corridor applications.

Part 2 of the BSM contains many optional data elements and is generally included in the BSM broadcast over the same DSRC channel when a triggering event or condition is present.

Because the BSM messages will be broadcast for V2V safety, it is reasonable to examine to what extent those messages alone can support mobility applications, and to what extent the same information, albeit packaged differently and perhaps sent over a different communications medium, could support mobility applications. This study provides an initial answer to these questions.

It is important to note that the fact that a data element is defined as an element of Part 2 of the BSM in the Society of Automotive Engineers (SAE) J2735 standard does not necessarily mean that it will be provided by vehicle manufacturers. Most of the Part 2 elements are defined as optional information in the standard. Moreover the list of data elements has been accurately described as a "wish list" of desired information. Some of the data elements are currently available on the vehicle's internal data bus and some are not. Some optional elements defined in the standard are easy to provide, while it may be infeasible to provide others (e.g., the BSM Part 2 element that provides the precipitation rate in tenths of grams per square meter per second).

Chapter 2: Approach

A very simplified model of Intelligent Transportation Systems was used to examine the information exchange needs. The model included three types of systems: roadside infrastructure, such as traffic signal controllers, "other" infrastructure, such as traffic management centers, and vehicles. Vehicles were further identified by type: light vehicle, transit vehicle, freight vehicle, emergency vehicle, and maintenance vehicle. This Model is shown in Figure 2-1. The analysis was focused on information that flowed to, from, or between vehicles (Links 1, 2, 3, 4, or 5, shown in red, in the figure).

Figure 2-1. Simplified ITS Model Used for Analysis

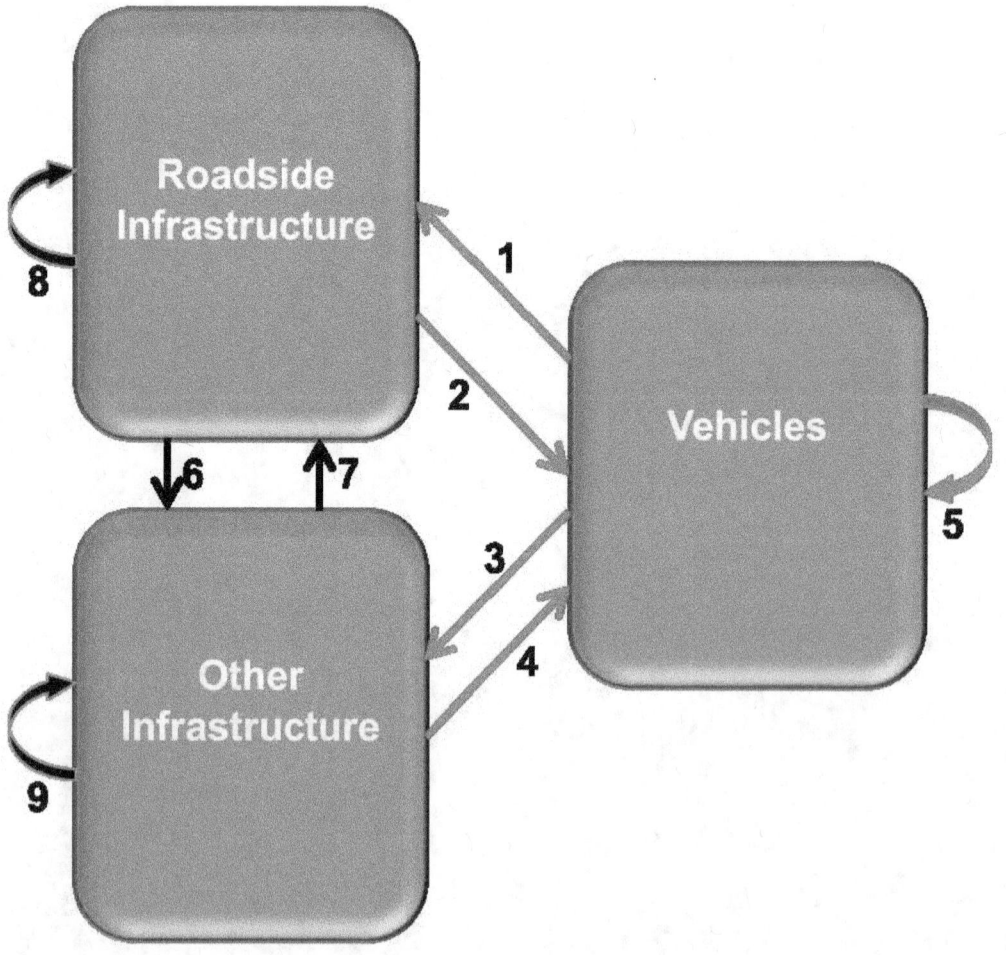

The information exchange requirements were determined at two levels. The lower level of detail was data elements, which are individual pieces of information, such as vehicle speed or "wipers on". The higher level was messages, which can be viewed for purposes of this analysis as a logical collection of data elements that might be bundled into a single message for some purpose (the BSM message, with and without Part 2, are examples of logical groupings used for V2V safety applications).

The analysis was conducted application by application. Twenty-nine of the thirty high priority mobility applications were analyzed. The exception was Emergency Vehicle Dynamic Route Guidance in the FRATIS bundle, as this application is being dropped from further development at this time. Appendix C lists these 30 applications. For each application, an assessment was made of what messages and which specific data elements would need to be sent to or from vehicles, to either directly or indirectly support the application. An example of an indirect need would be the Speed Harmonization application indirectly using weather data from vehicles, since weather is one of the factors used to determine the desired speed. A database was developed to track which messages and data elements were associated with which applications, which data elements went into each message type, and what systems the vehicle exchanged the messages with. A pictorial depiction of the database is shown in Figure 2-2.

Figure 2-2. Pictorial Depiction of the Database Used to Capture Information Exchange Needs

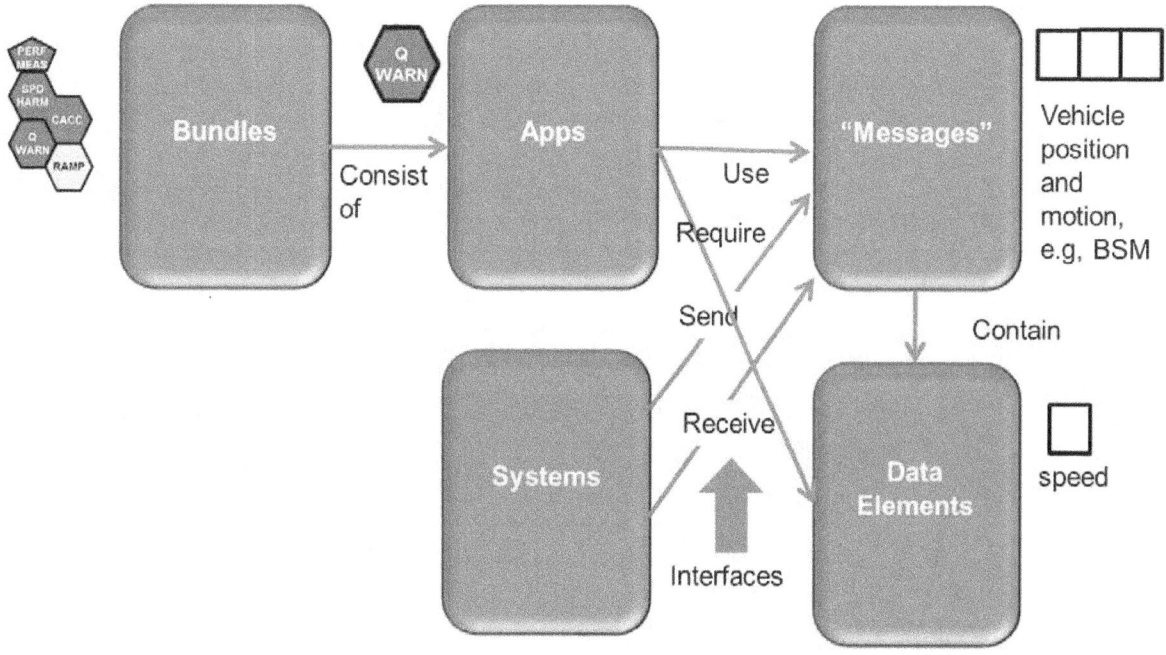

Scenarios

Five scenarios were defined, built around Parts 1 and 2 of the BSM, in order to determine the extent to which mobility applications could or could not be supported by BSM messages alone, and if the BSM messages are insufficient, what additional information needs to be exchanged. The five scenarios are:

1. BSM Part 1 via DSRC (only). This scenario assumes that the only messages flowing into or out of vehicles is the BSM Part 1 message, which is broadcast over DSRC. The infrastructure may receive BSM messages from vehicles, but does not send any messages to vehicles.

2. BSM Part 1 via DSRC plus other incoming messages. This expands scenario 1 to allow infrastructure systems to send other messages to vehicles (I2V messages), using any appropriate communications medium.

3. BSM Parts 1 and 2 via DSRC plus I2V messages. This expands scenario 2 by adding BSM messages containing Part 1 as well as Part 2, broadcast over DSRC.

4. BSM Parts 1 and 2 data elements bundled into one or more new messages and transmitted by other means, plus I2V messages. This is a much broader scenario than the previous three. It assumes that the only data that a vehicle can send out are the data elements found in parts 1 and 2 of the BSM, but that they may be bundled, cached, or aggregated in different ways, sent using different transmission strategies, and/or sent using other mobile wireless communications technologies, such as cellular radio.

5. BSM Parts 1 and 2 data elements bundled into one or more new messages and transmitted by other means plus additional incoming and outgoing messages (I2V, V2I, and V2V). This scenario is totally open, allowing vehicles to send and receive any data over any media.

All five scenarios include a common set of assumptions:

- Roadside DSRC radios are linked to central systems wherever necessary (e.g., DSRC can be used as one hop in a link between a vehicle and a traffic management center or other central system).

- Non-vehicular data sources in use today remain available (e.g, loop detectors, cellular probe data, Bluetooth detectors, etc.)

- Currently implemented communications systems (e.g., cell phones, transit radio systems) remain available.

- Vehicles have the capability to rebroadcast (relay) certain messages over DSRC. (The R.E.S.C.U.M.E. MAYDAY application is built around this capability, and other applications would benefit from it.

Caveats

This analysis was conducted to provide an assessment as rapidly as possible, based on very preliminary and incomplete definitions of each application. The findings will undoubtedly change to some extent as the concepts of operation and requirements for the applications are developed. In addition, the analysis was focused strictly on the information flows into and out of vehicles. No attempt was made to analyze information exchange requirements between central systems (e.g., a traffic management or transit management center) and roadside devices (e.g., a signal controller) or between central systems.

The analysis looked at messages that might be exchanged to support each application and the data elements that would go into those messages. However, the data elements list is incomplete. Routine data elements that do not relate to the actual application were not included. Examples of elements that were left out include log-in messages, acknowledgements, time stamps, and electronic signatures fields.

In many cases, a very small number of data elements would be needed to implement a very basic application, while a very large number of elements could potentially add varying degrees of value to the application.   In these cases, a judgment call was made, leaving out elements that, in the judgment of the analyst, would add only very marginal value (such as vehicle-based differential GPS corrections for the speed harmonization application. Similarly, optional BSM elements that are unlikely to be supported on vehicles for the foreseeable future were not included unless they were determined to be essential to an application.

This analsyis was based on the BSM message as defined in the November 2009 version of SAE J2735. This standard is currently being revised.

Chapter 3: Sample Analysis for Dynamic Speed Harmonization

Figure 3-1 shows the information exchange that occurs between vehicles and "other infrastructure" to enable the Dynamic Speed Harmonization (SPD-HARM) application. Other information flows between the roadside infrastructure and other infrastructure are not shown. The left hand side shows the message exchange, and the right hand lists the data elements contained in each message. The analysis shows that the vehicle needs to provide the information found in Part 1 of the BSM, and that some of the weather-related information found in Part 2 of the BSM would add value (although a system could be built using just existing infrastructure-based weather sensors). No other information is needed from the vehicle. However, if the BSM information is only available through DSRC broadcast at approximately 10 times per second, it would be necessary to install roadside DSRC systems wherever speed harmonization is desired. In practice, some method of caching and bundling BSM information on the vehicle, for transmission in one or more new messages over either DSRC or another mobile wireless medium, would be needed. In addition, vehicles must be capable of receiving and processing target lane and speed messages from the infrastructure.

A similar analysis was conducted for each of the high priority mobility applications.

Figure 3-1. Pictorial Depiction of the Database Used to Capture Information Exchange Needs

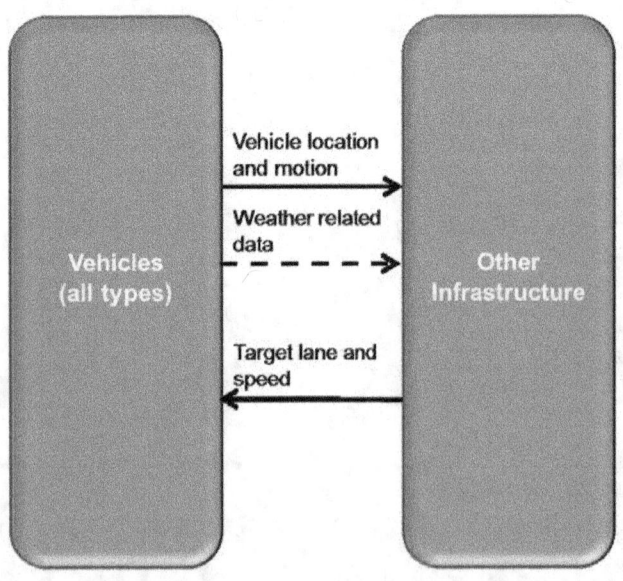

Messages and Data Elements
- Vehicle location and motion (contained in BSM Part 1)
  - Vehicle position, including accuracy
  - Vehicle speed
  - Vehicle acceleration
  - Vehicle size
- Weather related data (optional, all in BSM Part 2)
  - Antilock Break System active over 100 msec
  - Traction Control System active over 100 msec
  - Road coefficient of friction
  - Rain sensor
  - Light status changed
  - Wiper status changed
  - Light status
  - Wiper status
  - Ambient air temperature
  - Ambient barometric pressure
- Target lane and speed
  - Target speeds by lane, location, and possibly weight

Diagram labels: Vehicles (all types); Other Infrastructure; Vehicle location and motion; Weather related data; Target lane and speed

Chapter 4: Results and Conclusions

A summary of the types of vehicle-based data needed for each application bundle is provided below, followed by the overall results based on all scenarios and applications.

- **Enable ATIS: Enable Advanced Traveler Information Systems:** With the exception of traveler-provided information, e.g., destination and desired arrival time, the information contained in parts 1 and 2 of the BSM would provide all of the necessary vehicle information for the Enable ATIS applications. Although the Enable ATIS applications utilize the information found in the BSM, the information needs to be cached, bundled, and transmitted in one or more new messages, either using DSRC, another medium, or a combination of media.

- **INFLO (Integrated Network Flow Optimization):** The information contained in the two parts of the BSM message would provide all of the necessary vehicle information for the INFLO applications. Ramp Metering, Queue Warning in limited locations, and vehicle based Cooperative Adaptive Speed Control could function with the BSM messages sent as planned for safety applications, although vehicles would need to be able to receive and act on other messages sent to them. However other applications, such as Speed Harmonization, will require that the data be cached, bundled, and transmitted in one or more new messages, either using DSRC, another medium, or a combination of media.

  The BSM data elements of benefit to the INFLO applications are listed in Table 4-1. Each vehicle will also need to be capable of receiving other infrastructure to vehicle messages (e.g., a queue warning message).

Table 4-1. BSM Data Elements Used by INFLO Applications the Largest Number of Mobility Applications

BSM Part 1	BSM Part 2
Position (local 3D): • Latitude • Longitude • Elevation • Positional accuracy	Road coefficient of friction
Motion: • Transmission state • Speed • Heading • Steering wheel angle • Acceleration Set (4-way): this includes 3 axes of acceleration plus yaw rate	Rain sensor (called a Rain sensor in J2735, but it is a precipitation sensor. J2735 states "The "Rain Sensor" Probe Data Element is intended to inform Probe Data Users as to how hard it was raining/snowing…")
Brake System status	Traction Control System active over 100 msec
Vehicle size	Antilock Brake System active over 100 msec
	Date/time of obstacle detection
	Azimuth to obstacle on road
	Distance to obstacle on road
	Confidence-position
	Confidence-speed/heading/throttle
	Throttle position (percent)
	Confidence-time
	Trailer weight
	Recent or current hard breaking
	Level of brake application
	Vehicle data
	Hazard lights active

- **FRATIS (Freight Advanced Traveler Information Systems):** With the exception of information on desired routes and cargo information, e.g., load drop off time, the information contained in the two parts of the BSM would provide all of the necessary vehicle information for the FRATIS applications. Although the FRATIS applications utilize the information found in the BSM, the information needs to be cached, bundled, and transmitted in one or more new messages, either using DSRC, another medium, or a combination of media.

- **M-ISIG (Multimodal Intelligent Traffic Signal System):** The information contained in the two parts of the BSM would provide most of the necessary vehicle information for the M-ISIG applications. Additional transit-specific information (such as passenger count and schedule adherence) is needed from transit vehicles to support transit signal priority. Although the M-ISIG applications utilize the information found in both the BSM Part 1 and BSM Part 2 messages, the information needs to be cached, bundled, and transmitted in one or more new messages, either using DSRC, another medium, or a combination of media.

- **ICM (Next Generation Integrated Corridor Management):** The Next Generation ICM application makes use of the data found in parts 1 and 2 of the BSM. Although it uses the same information, the information needs to be grouped and transmitted cached, bundled, and transmitted in one or more new messages, either using DSRC, another medium, or a combination of media. The other ICM applications do not make use of the information found in the BSM messages. Additional information, such as account information and vehicle identification, would be needed from vehicles (but not necessarily from the vehicle data bus) to support electronic tolling and mileage-based user fees. It would also be of value to capture the type and amount of chemicals spread from maintenance vehicles to support the WX-MDSS application.

- **R.E.S.C.U.M.E. (Response, Emergency Staging and Communications, Uniform Management, and Evacuation):** These applications use the data found in parts 1 and 2 of the BSM. Although it uses the same information, the information needs to be cached, bundled, and transmitted in one or more new messages, either using DSRC, another medium, or a combination of media. In addition, the Mayday Relay application is expected to use additional vehicle-based crash data not found in the BSM message, such as occupant safety belt use, vehicle fuel type, vehicle resting position, and crash delta v (velocity).

- **IDTO (Integrated Dynamic Transit Operations):** The IDTO applications generally do not make use of the information found in the BSM messages. The sole exception is that Dynamic Ride-Sharing would utilize vehicle type information. Additional transit-specific information (such as passenger count and schedule adherence) is needed from transit and ride-sharing vehicles to support these applications.

Summarizing the results across the five scenarios defined in the approach section, and across all applications, the results of the analysis are shown in Table 4-2. Additional information beyond that directly obtained or sent to vehicles, such as information from travelers and other sensors, is a requirement for mobility applications and is assumed in all five scenarios.

Table 4-2. Summary of the ability of BSM Messages or other messages with BSM content to Support Mobility Applications

Scenario	Scenario Definition	Analysis Results
1	BSM Part 1 V2V via DSRC (only). This scenario assumes that the only messages flowing into or out of vehicles is the BSM Part 1 message, which is broadcast over DSRC. The infrastructure may receive BSM messages from vehicles, but does not send any messages to vehicles.	May be adequate to support a pure V2V approach to CACC; however this application would benefit from additional information found in the BSM Part 2 message. Inadequate to support any other mobility application
2	BSM Part 1 via DSRC plus other incoming messages. This expands scenario 1 to allow infrastructure systems to send other messages to vehicles (I2V messages), using any appropriate communications medium.	Supports a very limited number of applications, such as Ramp Metering and Queue Warning. Queue Warning would require roadside DSRC equipment wherever a queue warning is needed.
3	BSM Parts 1 and 2 via DSRC plus I2V messages. This expands scenario 2 by adding BSM messages containing Part 1 as well as Part 1, broadcast over DSRC.	Adequate for CACC. In principle, it could support other mobility applications; however, this is impractical, as it would require near-ubiquitous DSRC coverage along every mile of roadside.
4	BSM Parts 1 and 2 *data elements* bundled into one or more new messages and transmitted by other means, plus I2V messages. This is a much broader scenario than the previous three. It assumes that the only data that a vehicle can send out are the data elements found in parts 1 and 2 of the BSM, but that they may be bundled, cached, or aggregated in different ways, sent using different transmission strategies, and/or sent using other mobile wireless communications technologies, such as cellular radio.	Adequate to support many, but not all high priority mobility applications, provided the data can be cached and bundled in the vehicle for transmission, using either DSRC or other mobile wireless media (e.g., cellular data). Applications such as all IDTO applications, F-DRG, and MAYDAY require additional data from vehicles or vehicle operators.
5	BSM Parts 1 and 2 *data elements* bundled into one or more new messages and transmitted by other means plus additional incoming and outgoing messages (I2V, V2I, and V2V). This scenario is totally open, allowing vehicles to send and receive any data over any media.	Supports all mobility applications.

In summary, the Basic Safety Message (BSM), with Part 1 transmitted approximately 10 times per second over Dedicated Short Range Communications (DSRC), is useful for a limited subset of mobility applications, but is not solely sufficient for most applications, especially since complete roadway coverage using DSRC has never been envisioned as a feasible option. However, a subset of the BSM Part 1 and Part 2 data, if cached, bundled, and sent in another manner, adequately provides the vehicle-based information needed for most mobility applications. The major exception is crash-related data to support the MAYDAY application.

Information in the BSM part 1 and 2 messages is also needed for other mobility applications, but it needs to be cached, bundled, and transmitted in one or more new messages, either using DSRC, another medium, or a combination of media. The data is often needed for every stretch of roadway, but far less frequently. Since it is infeasible to provide continuous coverage of U.S. roadways using DSRC the data must be cached on-board the vehicle and then sent as a larger collection of data points. These new messages could be sent to roadside DSRC units spaced along the roadway (as in the original Vehicle Infrastructure Integration vision), sent via digital cellular, or through a combination of the two. If utilizing DSRC, the required level of deployment varies by application. For example, Ramp Metering, Cooperative Adaptive Cruise Control (if vehicle-based), and Queue Warning limited to high priority locations could be supported by selective spot deployment of roadside DSRC equipment. However other applications such as ATIS, Dynamic Speed Harmonization, or infrastructure-based CACC would require a relatively widespread, dense deployment as had originally been envisioned by the VII program.

The BSM *data elements* that are most widely used by mobility applications, albeit not in a 10 times per second BSM message, are the vehicle parameters found in Part 1 of the BSM and weather related data found in Part 2 of the BSM. This is shown in Table 4-3.

Table 4-3. BSM Data Elements Used by the Largest Number of Mobility Applications

BSM Part 1	BSM Part 2
Position (local 3D): • Latitude • Longitude • Elevation • Positional accuracy	Road coefficient of friction
Motion: • Transmission state • Speed • Heading • Steering wheel angle • Acceleration Set (4-way): this includes 3 axes of acceleration plus yaw rate	Rain sensor (called a Rain sensor in J2735, but it is a precipitation sensor. J2735 states "The "Rain Sensor" Probe Data Element is intended to inform Probe Data Users as to how hard it was raining/snowing…")
Vehicle size	Traction Control System active over 100 msec
	Antilock Brake System active over 100 msec
	Lights changed and Exterior lights (status)
	Wipers changed and wiper status
	Ambient air temperature
	Ambient air pressure
	Vehicle type (BSM currently only includes this for fleet vehicles)

There are two additional sets of vehicle information that are not found in parts 1 or 2 of the BSM but that may be of value to particular applications. First, the Mayday Relay and Incident Scene Pre-Arrival Staging and Guidance for Emergency Responders applications would benefit from crash-related data from the vehicle. Second, although outside the scope of this study, AERIS applications may derive value from additional variables such as fuel consumption and fuel efficiency. [Note: The Connected Eco Driving (ECO) application that is part of the Mulitpmodal Intelligent Traffic Signal Sytem (M-ISIG) bundle *was* included in the analysis, however as currently defined it does not require that information be sent from the vehicle]

If utilizing DSRC for communication, the amount of deployment needed varies by application. For example, Ramp Metering, Cooperative Adaptive Cruise Control (if vehicle-based), and Queue Warning limited to high priority locations could be supported by selective spot deployment of roadside DSRC equipment. However other applications (ATIS, Dynamic Speed Harmonization, or infrastructure-based CACC would require a relatively widespread, dense deployment as had originally been envisioned by the VII program.

It is important to note two additional items. First, with respect to BSM messages, the fact that a data element is defined as an element of Part 2 of the BSM in the Society of Automotive Engineers (SAE) J2735 standard does not necessarily mean that it will be provided by vehicle manufacturers. Most of the Part 2 elements are defined as optional information in the standard. Second, while this paper focusses on data from vehicles, it is important to keep in mind that transformative mobility applications will require data from travelers and other sensors, in addition to vehicle data.

APPENDIX A.   List of Acronyms

ABS	Antilock Braking System
AERIS	Applications for the Environment: Real-Time Information Synthesis
ASN.1	Abstract Syntax Notation One
ATIS	Advanced Traveler Information Systems
BSM	Basic Safety Message
CACC	Cooperative Adaptive Cruise Control
DE	Data Element
DF	Data Frame
DMA	Dynamic Mobility Applications
DOT	Department of Transportation
DRG	Dynamic Routing of Vehicles
D-RIDE	Dynamic Ridesharing
DR-OPT	Drayage Optimization
DSRC	Dedicated Short Range Communications
ECO	Connected Eco Driving
EFP	Multimodal Integrated Payment System
ETA	Estimated Time of Arrival
ETC	Electronic Toll Collection System
[EV] DRG	Dynamic Routing of Emergency Vehicles
EVAC	Emergency Communications and Evacuation
F-ATIS	Freight Real-time Traveler Information with Performance Monitoring
F-DRG	Freight Dynamic Route Guidance
FHWA	Federal Highway Administration
FRATIS	Freight Advanced Traveler Information Systems
FSP	Freight Signal Priority
GIS	Geographic Information System
GNSS	Global Navigation Satelite Systems
GPS	Global Positioning System
HAZMAT	Hazardous material.
I2V	Infrastructure to Vehicle
ICM	Integrated Corridor Management
IDTO	Integrated Dynamic Transit Operations

INC-ZONE	Incident Scene Workzone Alerts for Drivers and Workers
INFLO	Integrated Network Flow Optimization
I-SIG	Intelligent Traffic Signal System
ITIS	International Traveler Information Systems
ITS	Intelligent Transportation Systems
ITS JPO	Intelligent Transportation Systems Joint Program Office
M-ISIG	Multi-Modal Intelligent Traffic Signal System
MAYDAY	Mayday Relay
MDSS	Maintenance Decision Support System
NHTSA	National Highway Traffic Safety Administration
NTCIP	National Transportation Communications for ITS Protocol
PED-SIG	Mobile Accessible Pedestrian Signal System
Q-WARN	Queue Warning
RAMP	Next Generation Ramp Metering System
RDE	Research Data Exchange
RESP-STG	Incident Scene Pre-Arrival Staging and Guidance for Emergency Responders
RITA	Research and Innovative Technology Administration
RTCM	Radio Technical Commission for Maritime Services
S-PARK	Smart Park and Ride
SAE	Society of Automotive Engineers
SPD-HARM	Dynamic Speed Harmonization
T-CONNECT	Connection Protection
T-DISP	Dynamic Transit Operations
T-MAP	Universal Map Application
TSP	Transit Signal Priority
USDOT	United States Department of Transportation
V2I	Vehicle to Infrastructure
VII	Vehicle Infrastructure Integration
VMT	Mileage Based User Fee
WX	Weather
WX-INFO	Real-Time Route Specific Weather Information for Motorized and Non-Motorized Vehicles
WX-MDSS	Enhanced MDSS Communication

APPENDIX B. Vehicle Data Elements Needed to Support High Priority Mobility Applications

This table lists each data element that originates in a vehicle and is used by one or more mobility applications. The list is sorted by the type of vehicle that sends the message (all vehicles, emergency vehicles only, freight vehicles only, maintenance vehicles only, light vehicles only, or transit vehicles only). For each element, the third and fourth columns indicate if the element is found in Part 1 of the BSM message or Part 2 (or, if neither column is checked, in neither). The last column identifies whether or not the element may be useful in determining road weather conditions. This is included to show that most, but not all, desired Part 2 elements are weather-related.

System	Data Elements	BSM Part 1	BSM Part 2	Wx. Related
All Vehicles				
	Brake system status	✓		
	Position (local 3D)	✓		
	Vehicle size	✓		
	Motion	✓		
	Ambient air temperature		✓	✓
	Ambient air pressure		✓	✓
	Antilock Brake System active over 100 msec		✓	✓
	Exterior lights (status)		✓	✓
	Lights changed		✓	✓
	Rain sensor		✓	✓
	Road coefficient of friction		✓	✓
	Traction Control System active over 100 msec		✓	✓
	Wiper status		✓	✓
	Wipers changed		✓	✓
	Airbag deployment		✓	
	Azimuth to obstacle on the road		✓	
	Confidence-position		✓	
	Confidence-speed/heading/throttle		✓	
	Confidence-time		✓	
	Date/time of obstacle detection		✓	
	Distance to obstacle on road		✓	
	Hazard lights active		✓	

System	Data Elements	BSM Part 1	BSM Part 2	Wx. Related
	Level of brake application		✓	
	Recent or current hard braking		✓	
	Stop line violation		✓	
	Throttle position (percent)		✓	
	Vehicle data		✓	
	Vehicle type (fleet)		✓	
	Crash delta V			
	Estimated point of impact			
	Number of occupants			
	Occupant medical data			
	Occupant safety belt use			
	Owner ID			
	Toll payment			
	Vehicle fuel type			
	Vehicle ID			
	Vehicle log, including time, location, direction			
	Vehicle resting position			
Emergency Vehicles (only)				
	Light bar in use		✓	
	Public safety vehicle responding to emergency		✓	
	Siren in use		✓	
	Approach road to intersection			
	Intended turning movement at intersection			
Freight Vehicles(only)				
	Descriptive vehicle identifier		✓	
	Fleet Owner Code		✓	
	HAZMAT status		✓	
	Trailer weight		✓	
	Vehicle height		✓	
	Vehicle mass		✓	
	Vehicle placarded as HAZMAT carrier		✓	
	Vehicle type		✓	
	Destination and stops			

System	Data Elements	BSM Part 1	BSM Part 2	Wx. Related
	Electronic manifest			
	Load matching request			
	Pickup or dropoff time request			
Light Vehicles (only)				
	Cost			
	Departure location			
	Desired mode			
	Destination			
	Destination			
	ETA at destination			
	ETA for pickup			
	EVAC information request			
	Number of occupants in vehicle			
	Origin			
	Ride sharing response			
	Selected route and mode			
	Target arrival time			
	Target departure time			
Maint. Vehicles (only)				
	Maintenance activities			✓
	Segments and lanes plowed			✓
	Type and amount of road chemicals applied			✓
Transit Vehicles (only)				
	connection protection request			
	Current itinerary			
	Passenger count			
	Status versus schedule			
	Transit service type			

APPENDIX C. Data Elements by Application

This table lists the data element that originates in a vehicle and are used the mobility application listed in the second column. The list is sorted by DMA bundle (see Appendix C) and application. For each element, the fourth and fifth columns indicate if the element is found in Part 1 of the BSM message or Part 2 (or, if neither column is checked, in neither). The last column identifies whether or not the element may be useful in determining road weather conditions. This is included to show that most, but not all, desired Part 2 elements are weather-related.

Bundle Name	App Name	Data Element	In BSM Part 1	In BSM Part 2	Weather Related
Enable ATIS	ATIS	Motion	✓		
		Position (local 3D)	✓		
		Vehicle size	✓		
		Antilock Brake System active over 100 msec		✓	✓
		Traction Control System active over 100 msec		✓	✓
		Road coefficient of friction		✓	✓
		Rain sensor		✓	✓
		Lights changed		✓	✓
		Wipers changed		✓	✓
		Exterior lights (status)		✓	✓
		Wiper status		✓	✓
		Ambient air temperature		✓	✓
		Ambient air pressure		✓	✓
		Selected route and mode			
		Directions and times by mode			
		Departure location			
		Destination			
		Target departure time			
		Target arrival time			
Enable ATIS	S-PARK	Park and ride lot status info			

Appendix C. **Data Elements by Application**

Bundle Name	App Name	Data Element	In BSM Part 1	In BSM Part 2	Weather Related
Enable ATIS	T-MAP	Motion	✓		
		Position (local 3D)	✓		
		Vehicle size	✓		
		Location			
Enable ATIS	WX-INFO	Antilock Brake System active over 100 msec		✓	✓
		Traction Control System active over 100 msec		✓	✓
		Road coefficient of friction		✓	✓
		Rain sensor		✓	✓
		Lights changed		✓	✓
		Wipers changed		✓	✓
		Exterior lights (status)		✓	✓
		Wiper status		✓	✓
		Ambient air temperature		✓	✓
		Ambient air pressure		✓	✓
FRATIS	DR-OPT	Assigned load pickup time			
		Assigned load dropoff time			
		Change in pickup or dropoff time			
		Load matching response			
		Pickup or dropoff time request			
		Load matching request			
FRATIS	F-ATIS	Motion	✓		
		Position (local 3D)	✓		
		Antilock Brake System active over 100 msec		✓	✓
		Traction Control System active over 100 msec		✓	✓
		Road coefficient of friction		✓	✓
		Rain sensor		✓	✓

Joint Program Office
U.S. Department of Transportation, Research and Innovative Technology Administration

Vehicle Information Exchange Needs for Mobility Applications – Final

Appendix C. **Data Elements by Application**

Bundle Name	App Name	Data Element	In BSM Part 1	In BSM Part 2	Weather Related
		Lights changed		✓	✓
		Wipers changed		✓	✓
		Exterior lights (status)		✓	✓
		Wiper status		✓	✓
		Ambient air temperature		✓	✓
		Ambient air pressure		✓	✓
		Weather info for freight			✓
		Vehicle data		✓	
		Recent or current hard braking		✓	
		Confidence-time		✓	
		Confidence-position		✓	
		Confidence-speed/heading/throttle		✓	
		Freight routing with travel times			
		Incident alerts			
		Road closure info			
		Work zone info			
		Freight routing restictions			
		Regulatory and enforcement info			
		Info on concierge and maintenance services and locations			
FRATIS	F-DRG	Antilock Brake System active over 100 msec		✓	✓
		Traction Control System active over 100 msec		✓	✓
		Road coefficient of friction		✓	✓
		Rain sensor		✓	✓
		Lights changed		✓	✓
		Wipers changed		✓	✓
		Exterior lights (status)		✓	✓

Joint Program Office
U.S. Department of Transportation, Research and Innovative Technology Administration

Vehicle Information Exchange Needs for Mobility Applications – Final

Appendix C. Data Elements by Application

Bundle Name	App Name	Data Element	In BSM Part 1	In BSM Part 2	Weather Related
		Wiper status		✓	✓
		Ambient air temperature		✓	✓
		Ambient air pressure		✓	✓
		Vehicle placarded as HAZMAT carrier		✓	
		Vehicle height		✓	
		Vehicle mass		✓	
		HAZMAT status		✓	
		Vehicle type (fleet)		✓	
		Descriptive vehicle identifier		✓	
		Fleet Owner Code		✓	
		Freight route guidance update			
		Freight route guidance response			
		Destination and stops			
ICM	ETC	Toll payment request			
		Toll payment			
		Toll payment confirmation			
ICM	VMT	Vehicle type (fleet)		✓	
		Vehicle ID			
		Owner ID			
		Vehicle log, including time, location, direction			
ICM	WX-MDSS	Road treatment recommendations			
		Maintenance activities			
		Type and amount of road chemicals applied			✓
IDTO	D-RIDE	Vehicle type (fleet)		✓	
		ETA for pickup			
		ETA at destination			

Joint Program Office
U.S. Department of Transportation, Research and Innovative Technology Administration

Vehicle Information Exchange Needs for Mobility Applications – Final

Appendix C. Data Elements by Application

Bundle Name	App Name	Data Element	In BSM Part 1	In BSM Part 2	Weather Related
		Target departure time			
		Destination			
		Target arrival time			
		Amount willing to pay			
		Departure location			
		Cost			
		Number of occupants in vehicle			
IDTO	T-CONNECT	Current itinerary			
		Connection protection response			
		Connection protection update			
		List of number of passengers by route			
		Passenger count			
		Schedule update			
		Status versus scehdule			
		Updated schedules			
IDTO	T-DISP	Passenger count			
		Revised routes, including timing			
		schedule updates			
		Status versus schedule			
		Itinerary			
		Target time(s) of arrival			
		Target time(s) of departure			
		Location			
		Status			
		Request being responded to			
		Pickup location(s)			

Joint Program Office
U.S. Department of Transportation, Research and Innovative Technology Administration

Vehicle Information Exchange Needs for Mobility Applications – Final

Appendix C. **Data Elements by Application**

Bundle Name	App Name	Data Element	In BSM Part 1	In BSM Part 2	Weather Related
		Pickup time(s)			
		Revised routes, including timing			
		Destination time(s)			
		Vehicle dispatched			
		Schedule			
INFLO	CACC	Vehicle size	✓		
		Brake system status	✓		
		Motion	✓		
		Position (local 3D)	✓		
		Road coefficient of friction		✓	✓
		Rain sensor		✓	✓
		Traction Control System active over 100 msec		✓	✓
		Antilock Brake System active over 100 msec		✓	✓
		Date/time of obstacle detection		✓	
		Azimuth to obstacle on the road		✓	
		Confidence-position		✓	
		Confidence-speed/heading/throttle		✓	
		Throttle position (percent)		✓	
		Trailer weight		✓	
		Confidence-time		✓	
		Recent or current hard braking		✓	
		Level of brake application		✓	
		Vehicle data		✓	
		Distance to obstacle on road		✓	
		Hazard lights active		✓	
		Geocoded road segment			

Joint Program Office
U.S. Department of Transportation, Research and Innovative Technology Administration

Vehicle Information Exchange Needs for Mobility Applications – Final

Appendix C. **Data Elements by Application**

Bundle Name	App Name	Data Element	In BSM Part 1	In BSM Part 2	Weather Related
		Gap recommendation by vehicle type			
INFLO	Q-WARN	Motion	✓		
		Position (local 3D)	✓		
		Type (moving/fixed) or speed of end of queue			
		Location of End of Queue (including lane)			
INFLO	RAMP	Position (local 3D)	✓		
		Motion	✓		
		Status of ramp meter			
INFLO	SPD-HARM	Motion	✓		
		Exterior lights (status)		✓	✓
		Ambient air temperature		✓	✓
		Antilock Brake System active over 100 msec		✓	✓
		Ambient air pressure		✓	✓
		Wiper status		✓	✓
		Lights changed		✓	✓
		Wipers changed		✓	✓
		Rain sensor		✓	✓
		Road coefficient of friction		✓	✓
		Traction Control System active over 100 msec		✓	✓
		Level of brake application		✓	
		SPaT data			
		target speeds by lane (list)			
M-ISIG	FSP	Motion	✓		
		Position (local 3D)	✓		
		Road coefficient of friction			✓
		Rain sensor			✓

Joint Program Office
U.S. Department of Transportation, Research and Innovative Technology Administration

Vehicle Information Exchange Needs for Mobility Applications – Final

Appendix C. Data Elements by Application

Bundle Name	App Name	Data Element	In BSM Part 1	In BSM Part 2	Weather Related
		Lights changed		✓	✓
		Wipers changed		✓	✓
		Exterior lights (status)		✓	✓
		Wiper status		✓	✓
		Ambient air temperature		✓	✓
M-ISIG	I-SIG	Motion	✓		
		Position (local 3D)	✓		
		Vehicle size	✓		
		Antilock Brake System active over 100 msec		✓	✓
		Traction Control System active over 100 msec		✓	✓
		Road coefficient of friction		✓	✓
		Rain sensor		✓	✓
		Lights changed		✓	✓
		Wipers changed		✓	✓
		Exterior lights (status)		✓	✓
		Wiper status		✓	✓
		Ambient air temperature		✓	✓
		Ambient air pressure		✓	✓
		Weather info for freight		✓	✓
		Vehicle type (fleet)		✓	
		Stop line violation		✓	
M-ISIG	PED-SIG	Public safety vehicle responding to emergency		✓	
		Light bar in use		✓	
		Siren in use		✓	
		Approach road to intersection			
		Intended turning movement at intersection			

Appendix C. **Data Elements by Application**

Bundle Name	App Name	Data Element	In BSM Part 1	In BSM Part 2	Weather Related
		Pedestrian location			
		Pedestrian intended crossing direction			
		Crossing status			
		Crossing heading correction			
M-ISIG	PREEMPT	Motion	✓		
		Position (local 3D)	✓		
		Public safety vehicle responding to emergency		✓	
		Approach road to intersection			
		Intended turning movement at intersection			
M-ISIG	TSP	Position (local 3D)	✓		
		Motion	✓		
		Passenger count			
		Transit service type			
		Approach road to intersection			
		Intended turning movement at intersection			
		Status versus scehdule			
R.E.S.C.U.M.E.	EVAC	Position (local 3D)	✓		
		Vehicle dispatched			
		Schedule			
		Origin			
		Destination			
		Desired mode			
		Route information			
		Evacuation routes information			
		Road conditions			
		Traffic reports			

Appendix C. Data Elements by Application

Bundle Name	App Name	Data Element	In BSM Part 1	In BSM Part 2	Weather Related
		EVAC information request			
		Locations for lodging, food, water, fuel, cash machines, etc.			
		Special needs			
		EVAC help response			
R.E.S.C.U.M.E.	INC-ZONE	Motion	✓		
		Position (local 3D)	✓		
		Lane closure information			
		Incident or work zone speed limit			
R.E.S.C.U.M.E.	MAYDAY	Position (local 3D)	✓		
		Airbag deployment		✓	
		Vehicle type (fleet)		✓	
		Crash delta V			
		Occupant safety belt use			
		Number of occupants			
		Estimated point of impact			
		Vehicle fuel type			
		Vehicle resting position			
		Occupant medical data			
		Electronic manifest			
R.E.S.C.U.M.E.	RESP-STG	Position (local 3D)	✓		
		Motion	✓		
		Vehicle size	✓		
		Antilock Brake System active over 100 msec		✓	✓
		Traction Control System active over 100 msec		✓	✓
		Road coefficient of friction		✓	✓
		Rain sensor		✓	✓

Joint Program Office
U.S. Department of Transportation, Research and Innovative Technology Administration

Vehicle Information Exchange Needs for Mobility Applications – Final

Appendix C. **Data Elements by Application**

Bundle Name	App Name	Data Element	In BSM Part 1	In BSM Part 2	Weather Related
		Lights changed		✓	✓
		Wipers changed		✓	✓
		Exterior lights (status)		✓	✓
		Wiper status		✓	✓
		Ambient air temperature		✓	✓
		Ambient air pressure		✓	✓
		Vehicle type (fleet)		✓	
		Airbag deployment		✓	
		Hazard lights active		✓	
		Recent or current hard braking		✓	
		Crash delta V			
		Occupant safety belt use			
		Number of occupants			
		Estimated point of impact			
		Vehicle fuel type			
		Vehicle resting position			
		Occupant medical data			
		Electronic manifest			
		Staging plans			
		Satellite imagery and GIS data			
		Still and video images			
		Road conditions			
		Traffic reports			
		Info on emergency centers			
		Weather information, including winds			
		Segments and lanes plowed			✓

APPENDIX D. List of High Priority Mobility Applications by Application Bundle

Enable ATIS: Enable Advanced Traveler Information Systems • ATIS: Multi-Modal Real-Time Traveler Information • S-PARK: Smart Park and Ride • T-MAP: Universal Map Application • WX-INFO: Real-Time Route Specific Weather Information for Motorized and Non-Motorized Vehicles	**INFLO:** Integrated Network Flow Optimization • CACC: Cooperative Adaptive Cruise Control • Q-WARN: Queue Warning • RAMP: Next Generation Ramp Metering System • SPD-HARM: Dynamic Speed Harmonization
FRATIS: Freight Advanced Traveler Information Systems • **DR-OPT:** Drayage Optimization • **[EV] DRG:** Dynamic Routing of Emergency Vehicles • **F-ATIS:** Freight Real-Time Traveler Information with Performance Monitoring • **F-DRG:** Freight Dynamic Route Guidance	**M-ISIG:** Multimodal Intelligent Traffic Signal System • **ECO:** Connected Eco Driving • **FSP:** Freight Signal Priority • **I-SIG:** Intelligent Traffic Signal System • **PED-SIG:** Mobile Accessible Pedestrian Signal System • **PREEMPT:** Emergency Vehicle Preemption with Proximity Warning • **TSP:** Transit Signal Priority
ICM: Next Generation Integrated Corridor Management • **ETC:** Electronic Toll Collection System • **ICM:** Next generation Integrated Corridor Management • **WX-MDSS:** Enhanced MDSS Communication • **VMT:** Mileage Based User Fee	**R.E.S.C.U.M.E.:** Response, Emergency Staging and Communications, Uniform Management, and Evacuation • **EVAC:** Emergency Communications and Evacuation • **INC-ZONE:** Incident Scene Work Zone Alerts for Drivers and Workers • **MAYDAY:** Mayday Relay • **RESP-STG:** Incident Scene Pre-Arrival Staging and Guidance for Emergency Responders
IDTO: Integrated Dynamic Transit Operations • **D-RIDE:** Dynamic Ridesharing • **EFP:** Multimodal Integrated Payment System • **T-CONNECT:** Connection Protection • **T-DISP:** Dynamic Transit Operations	

APPENDIX E. The Basic Safety Message (Parts 1 and 2)

The Basic Safety Message (BSM) is one of a set of messages defined in the Society of Automotive Engineers (SAE) Standard J2735, *Dedicated Short Range Communications (DSRC) Message Set Dictionary.* Each message in the standard, including the BSM, is made up of a set of *data frames,* which in turn are made up either of other data frames or *data elements.* Data elements are atomic, and are not further subdivided. In a few cases, the text, formal name, and ASN.1 definition found in J2739 provides conflicting information as to whether or not an item is a data frame or data element. For purposes of this analysis, it doesn't really matter.

The BSM consists of two parts. Part 1 is sent in every BSM message. Part 2 consists of a large set of optional elements. Not all elements are available from all vehicles, and which elements are sent, if available, will be based on event criteria that are not specified in J2735.

The table below lists the major data frames and data elements. It is not decomposed completely into data elements, as this would result in a very long list running many pages. Each item in the list is identified as either a data frame (DF) or data element (DE). If the data frame is not decomposed in this appendix, additional information on its content can be found in SAE J2735. "Administrative" components such as message ID number and time stamps are not listed in order to keep the list concise and emphasize the informational content that may be of value to mobility applications.

Part 1 (mandatory)

- Position (local 3D) (DF)

  - Latitude (DE)
  - Longitude (DE)
  - Elevation (DE)
  - Positional accuracy (DE)

- Motion (DF)

  - Transmission and speed (DF)
    - Transmission state (DE)
    - Speed (DE)
  - Heading (DE)
  - Steering wheel angle (DE)
  - Acceleration set (DF)
    - Longitudinal acceleration (DE)
    - Lateral acceleration (DE)
    - Vertical acceleration (DE)
    - Yaw rate (DE)

- Brake system status (DF)

  - Brake applied status (DE)
  - Brake status not available (DE)
  - Traction control state (DE)
  - Antilock brake status (DE)
  - Stability control status (DE)
  - Brake boost applied (DE)
  - Auxiliary brake status (DE)

- Vehicle size (DF)

  - Vehicle width (DE)
  - Vehicle length (DE)

Part 2 (all elements optional, sent according to criteria to be established)

- Vehicle safety extension (DF)
  - Event flags (DE) – A data element consisting of single bit event flags:
    - Hazard lights
    - Intersection stop line violation
    - ABS activated
    - Traction control loss
    - Stability control activated
    - Hazardous materials
    - Emergency response
    - Hard braking
    - Lights changed
    - Wipers changed
    - Flat tire
    - Disabled vehicle
    - Air bag deployment
  - Path history (DF)
    - Full position vector (DF)
      - Date and time stamp (DE)
      - Longitude (DE)
      - Latitude (DE)
      - Elevation (DE)
      - Heading (DE)
      - Transmission and speed (DF) – same as in Part 1
      - Positional accuracy (DE)
      - Time confidence (DE)
      - Position confidence set (DF)
        - Position confidence (DE)
        - Elevation confidence (DE)
      - Speed and heading and throttle confidence (DF)
        - Speed confidence (DE)
        - Heading confidence (DE)
        - Throttle confidence (DE)
    - GPS status (DE)
    - Count (DE) – number of "crumbs" in the history
    - Crumb data – set of one of 10 possible path history point set types, consisting of various combinations of:
      - Latitudinal offset from current position (DE)
      - Longitudinal offset from current position (DE)
      - Elevation offset from current position (DE)
      - Time offset from the current time (DE)
      - Accuracy (DF) – See J2735 standard for more information
      - Heading (DE) – NOT an offset, but absolute heading

- Transmission and speed (DF) – same as in Part 1, NOT an offset
- Path Prediction (DF)
  - Radius of curve (DE)
  - Confidence (DE)
- RTCM Package (DF) – RTCM (Radio Technical Commission for Maritime Services) is a standardized format for GPS messages, including differential correction messages. J2735 states "The RTCMPackage data frame is used to convey a select sub-set of the RTCM messages (message types 1001 TO 1032) which deal with differential corrections between users. Encapsulates messages are those defined in RTCM Standard 10403.1 for Differential GNSS (Global Navigation Satellite Systems)Services -Version 3 adopted on October 27, 2006 and its successors.
  - Full position vector (DF) – see full contents above under Path history
  - RTCM header (DF)
    - GPS status
    - Antenna offset
  - GPS data – see SAE J2735 and RTCM standards for more information

- Vehicle status (DF)

  - Exterior lights (DE)
  - Light bar in use (DE)
  - Wipers (DF)
    - Wiper status front (DE)
    - Wiper rate (front) (DE)
    - Wiper status rear (DE)
    - Wiper rate (rear) (DE)
  - Brake system status (DF) – same as in Part 1
  - Braking pressure (DE)
  - Roadway friction (DE)
  - Sun sensor (DE)
  - Rain sensor (DE)
  - Ambient air temperature (DE)
  - Ambient pressure (DE)
  - Steering, sequence of:
    - Steering wheel angle (DE)
    - Steering wheel angle confidence (DE)
    - Steering wheel angle rate of change (DE)
    - Driving wheel angle (DE)
  - Acceleration set (DF) – same as in Part 1
  - Vertical acceleration threshold (DE)
  - Yaw rate confidence (DE)
  - Acceleration confidence (DE)
  - Confidence set (DF)
    - Acceleration confidence (DE)
    - Speed confidence (speed, heading, and throttle confidences (DF)

    - Time confidence (DE)

- o Position confidence set (DF)
- o Steering wheel angle confidence (DE)
- o Throttle confidence (DE)
- Object data, sequence of:
  - o Obstacle distance (DE)
  - o Obstacle direction (DE)
  - o Time obstacle detected (DE)
- Full position vector (DF) – see contents under path history
- Throttle position (DE)
- Speed and heading and throttle confidence (DF) – same as above under "Full position vector"
- Speed confidence (DE) – same as above under "Speed and heading and throttle confidence"
- Vehicle data (referred to as a "complex type" in J2735, rather than an element or frame)
  - o Vehicle height (DE)
  - o Bumper heights (DF)
    - Bumber height front (DE)
    - Bumper height rear (DE)
  - o Vehicle mass (DE)
  - o Trailer weight (DE)
  - o Vehicle type (DE)
- Vehicle identity (DF)
  - o Descriptive name (DE) – typically only used for debugging
  - o VIN string (DE)
  - o Owner code (DE)
  - o Temporary ID (DE)
  - o Vehicle type (DE)
  - o Vehicle class (drawn from ITIS code standard)
- J1939 data (DF)
  - o Tire conditions (DF) – see J2735 standard for list of data elements
  - o Vehicle weight by axle (DF) – see J2735 standard for list of data elements
  - o Trailer weight (DE)
  - o Cargo weight (DE)
  - o Steering axle temperature (DE)
  - o Drive axle location (DE)
  - o Drive axle lift air pressure (DE)
  - o Drive axle temperature (DE)
  - o Dive axle lube pressure (DE)
  - o Steering axle lube pressure (DE)
- Weather report, defined as a sequence of the following:
  - o Is raining (DE) – defined in NTCIP standard
  - o Rain rate (DE) – defined in NTCIP standard
  - o Precipitation situation (DE) – defined in NTCIP standard
  - o Solar radiation (DE) – defined in NTCIP standard
  - o Mobile friction (DE) – defined in NTCIP standard
- GPS status (DE)

U.S. Department of Transportation
ITS Joint Program Office-HOIT
1200 New Jersey Avenue, SE
Washington, DC 20590

Toll-Free "Help Line" 866-367-7487
www.its.dot.gov

FHWA-JPO-12-021

U.S. Department of Transportation

Research and Innovative Technology Administration